Alex Rodriguez

By Jeffrey Zuehlke

AMAZING ATHLETES

LERNERSPORTS / Minneapolis

This book is available in two editions:
Library binding by LernerSports
Soft cover by First Avenue Editions
Imprints of Lerner Publishing Group
241 First Avenue North
Minneapolis, MN 55401 U.S.A.

Website address: www.lernerbooks.com

Library of Congress Cataloging-in-Publication Data

Zuehlke, Jeffrey, 1968–
    Alex Rodriguez / by Jeffrey Zuehlke.
        p.   cm. — (Amazing athletes)
    Includes index.
    ISBN: 0–8225–2427–9 (lib. bdg. : alk. paper)
    ISBN: 0–8225–2311–6 (pbk. : alk. paper)
    1. Rodriguez, Alex, 1975– —Juvenile literature. 2. Baseball players—United States—Biography—Juvenile literature. [1. Rodriguez, Alex, 1975– 2. Baseball players. 3. Dominican Americans—Biography.] I. Title. II. Series.
    GV865.R62Z84 2005
    796.357'092—dc22   2003026218

Manufactured in the United States of America
1 2 3 4 5 6 – DP – 10 09 08 07 06 05

TABLE OF CONTENTS

Alex takes a practice swing before stepping up to the plate.

THE BEST

Alex Rodriguez stepped up to the plate. The New York Yankees third baseman gripped the bat tightly and waited for the pitch.

Alex's Yankees were playing the Minnesota Twins in Game Four of the 2004 American League Division Series. New York was leading Minnesota in the series, two games to one. The

Yankees needed to win this game to win the series. Winning the series would let them move on to play in the American League Championship Series (ALCS).

The Twins had taken an early 5–1 lead in this exciting game. But the Yankees had come back. The game was tied 5–5 going into extra innings.

The Yankees celebrate beating the Twins in Game Two. The win tied the division series.

The Twins brought in Kyle Lohse in the eighth inning to stop the Yankees.

Twins pitcher Kyle Lohse threw a blazing fastball toward the plate. Alex swung the bat. CRACK! Alex sent a screaming **line drive** down the third base line.

Twins third baseman Corey Koskie had no chance to stop the hard-hit ball. It scooted down into the left field corner. Alex sprinted into second base with a **double.** The Yankees were two bases away from taking the lead!

Yankee right fielder Gary Sheffield came up to bat. After a few pitches, Alex took off for third base. He covered the distance in just a few seconds. Alex slid in with a **stolen base.** He was just 90 feet away from scoring the winning run!

Moments later, Lohse threw a pitch that bounced in the dirt in front of home plate. Twins catcher Pat Borders couldn't grab it. The ball bounced away from him. **Wild pitch!** Alex saw his chance and sprinted toward home. He clapped his hands as he stepped on the plate. The Yankees took the lead, 6–5.

Alex steals third base behind Corey Koskie. The steal put Alex in scoring position.

Alex (number 13) and Derek Jeter celebrate the Yankee win.

Yankees ace pitcher Mariano Rivera kept the Twins from scoring in the bottom of the inning. The Yankees won the game and the series. Thanks to Alex's excellent hitting and baserunning, the Yankees were one step closer to the **World Series.** After the game, Alex's teammates praised him.

"He is the best," said Gary Sheffield.

Alex was born in New York City. His family lived in the Washington Heights area, which includes Fort Tryon Park.

GROWING UP

Alex Rodriguez was born in New York City on July 27, 1975. He was the youngest of three children. Alex's father, Victor Rodriguez, had played professional baseball. Victor taught Alex how to swing a bat and how to catch and throw the ball. Soon Alex and his friends were playing baseball every day.

When Alex was eight years old, his family moved to Kendall, Florida, near Miami. Alex played baseball whenever he could. He practiced hitting, fielding, and baserunning. He dreamed of being a **Major League Baseball (MLB)** player. He hoped to play in the World Series one day.

Alex grew quickly. Soon he was taller, stronger, and faster than most kids his age. Alex often played with athletes a few years older than he was. Playing with bigger kids was a challenge. It made Alex a better player.

Victor Rodriguez was born in the Dominican Republic, a country in the Caribbean Sea. Baseball is very popular there.

Life was going great for Alex until just after his ninth birthday. At that time, his father left the family. Victor Rodriguez moved away and never came back.

As a kid, Alex spent a lot of time playing sports at the Boys & Girls Club near his home in Florida. As an adult, Alex still spends a lot of time at the Boys & Girls Club. He has given lots of his time and money to help support the organization.

Alex was a good student in spite of family problems.

Alex was heartbroken. But playing baseball helped him feel better. Meanwhile, Alex's mother, Lourdes, worked hard to take care of Alex, his sister, Susy, and his brother, Joe.

Lourdes encouraged Alex to keep playing baseball and to practice hard. She also made sure that Alex worked in school. Alex loved learning. He studied and earned good grades.

Lourdes told Alex not to brag about his baseball talents. She taught Alex to be polite and treat people with respect.

Alex played shortstop for Westminster Christian School in Miami. The small high school had one of the best high school baseball teams in the country.

Alex graduated from Westminster in 1993. The school named him to its baseball Hall of Fame.

AMAZING ATHLETE

As a teenager, Alex was one of the best high school baseball players in the United States. Scouts from MLB teams came to watch him play. Scouts liked the way he practiced hard, studied hard, and treated people with respect.

At first, Alex was unhappy that the Seattle Mariners had drafted him. The Mariners had been a losing team for many years. But he soon became excited about playing with Mariner superstars Ken Griffey Jr., Edgar Martinez, Randy Johnson, and Jay Buhner.

In June 1993, the Seattle Mariners picked Alex first in the MLB **draft.** Alex's dream of being a major league ballplayer was close to coming true. But he would have to work hard to earn a spot on the team.

Alex started the 1994 season in the **minor leagues.** He quickly showed how good he was and how fast he was learning. He hit the ball hard and made big plays in the field. By the middle of the season, the Mariners wanted Alex to play for the big league club.

Alex played his first major league game on July 7, 1994. He was just 18 years old. Alex played for the Mariners for 26 days. Sometimes he played great. Other times he made mistakes. Alex still had a lot to learn. The Mariners sent him back to the minor leagues to get better.

Alex is only the third 18-year-old since 1900 to play shortstop in the major leagues.

In 1995, Alex bounced up and down between the minor leagues and the Mariners. He became unhappy at times. Alex wanted to stay with the Mariners, but he was still young and needed to improve. At the end of the season, he promised to work extra hard to become the Mariners starting shortstop the next season.

Alex worked hard to stay on the Mariners. But after being sent down to the minor leagues three times, he almost quit.

Alex improved his batting and fielding skills in 1996.

SUPERSTAR

That winter, Alex exercised and practiced six days a week. In 1996, he arrived at spring training in top shape.

Alex's hard work paid off. He quickly became one of the league's toughest hitters, with a .358 batting average. He slugged 36 home runs and 54 doubles. He scored 141 runs and collected 123 runs batted in (RBI). Alex made dozens of great plays in the field too.

Alex was selected to his first American League All-Star Team. His teammates and fans gave him a nickname, A-Rod. Alex became one of the most popular players in baseball.

Alex had another super year in 1997. In fact, the whole Mariner team did well. They won their division, earning a spot in the playoffs. But the Mariners lost to the Baltimore Orioles in the division series. Alex was disappointed

Alex signs autographs for Seattle fans.

but planned to practice hard and have another great season.

In 1998, Alex became only the third "40–40" player in major league history. He hit 42 home runs and stole 46 bases. The next season, he became the first shortstop to hit more than 40 home runs two years in a row.

In 2000, Alex made it three years in a row, hitting 41 home runs. He also led the Mariners to the playoffs again. They beat the Chicago White Sox in the division series, but they lost to the New York Yankees in the ALCS.

By this time, many people were calling Alex the best player in baseball. Some were saying he might be the best baseball player *ever*.

Baseball experts call Alex a "five-tool player." That means he's great at the five most important baseball skills. He can run fast, catch the ball well, throw well, hit for a high batting average, and hit for power.

Alex tries not to let all of the praise go to his head. He knows he has talent. But he also knows he has to work hard to be the best. "He's a down to earth guy," said one of his teammates. "He works [hard] just like everybody else."

As he became more famous, Alex stayed focused on his game.

Alex liked his Mariner teammates. But he was ready for a change.

After the 2000 season, Alex became a **free agent.** He could choose to play with any team that wanted him. The Mariners, New York Mets, Texas Rangers, and several other teams wanted Alex to play for them.

Alex chose the Texas Rangers. He signed a contract to play for the Rangers for 10 years. In return, the team agreed to pay Alex $252 million over 10 years. It was the richest contract in sports history!

Actor Mark Wahlberg, Alex, and Ken Griffey Jr. *(back row left to right)* meet with members of the Boys & Girls Clubs of America.

GREAT PLAYER, GREAT PERSON

Alex knows he's lucky to be so rich and successful. He tries to help others as often as he can. He works with the Boys & Girls Clubs in Miami, Dallas, and New York City. He has given money to help build ballparks and gyms, where kids can play sports. Alex also visits schools. He tells students to work hard to achieve their dreams.

Alex had three super seasons with the Rangers. In 2001, he led the American League in home runs with 52. He played in every game and made many great plays at shortstop. In 2002, Alex smacked 57 home runs—tops in the league again. The next season, he led the American League in home runs for the third year in a row, hitting 47. At the end of the 2003 season, Alex was voted the American League's Most Valuable Player.

Alex talks with Cal Ripkin Jr. during the 2001 All-Star Game. Ripkin has been one of Alex's favorite players since childhood.

But even though Alex played well, the Rangers struggled. The team finished in last place in 2003. Alex loved the Texas fans and his Ranger teammates, but he wanted to play on a winning team. He wanted to make it to the World Series.

Before the 2004 season, the New York Yankees offered to trade for Alex. But there was one problem. The Yankees already had a great shortstop, Derek Jeter. Would Alex change positions to play for the Yankees?

Alex worked hard for the Rangers. But he wanted to play in the World Series.

Wearing his new Yankees uniform, Alex poses for photographs with his wife, Cynthia. Alex joined the Yankees in February 2004.

Alex quickly agreed to the switch. He became the new third baseman for the Yankees. His teammates included superstars Jason Giambi, Bernie Williams, Mike Mussina, Gary Sheffield, Hideki Matsui, Mariano Rivera, and one of Alex's best friends, Derek Jeter.

"I can't express . . . how grateful I am to be a Yankee," Alex wrote before the 2004 season started. "I just don't have the words for it."

With Alex leading the way, the Yankees had a super season. They won 101 games to finish in first place in their division. Alex hit 36 home runs and knocked in 106 RBI.

Derek Jeter *(left)*, Alex, and Jason Giambi joke while doing exercises at spring training in 2004. The Yankees train at Legends Field in Tampa, Florida.

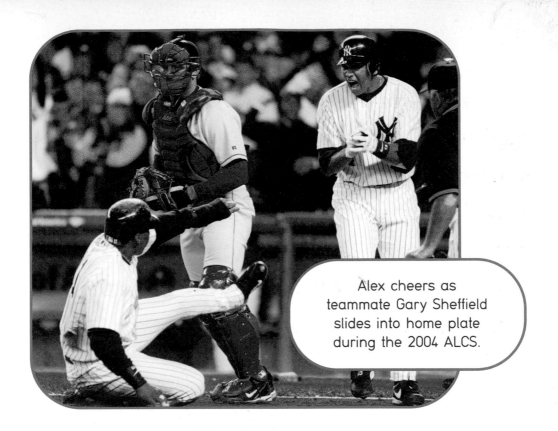

Alex cheers as teammate Gary Sheffield slides into home plate during the 2004 ALCS.

In the division series, the Yankees defeated the Minnesota Twins in four exciting games. Then Alex and his teammates moved on to play the Boston Red Sox in the ALCS. The Yankees started out the series with a bang. They beat the Red Sox in the first three games. In Game Three, Alex hit a home run and the Yankees ended up winning 19–7!

The Yankees were one game away from going to the World Series. They just had to beat the Red Sox one more time. But the Sox hung on and won the next four games. Alex's season ended in disappointment.

Losing to the Red Sox was tough. But Alex will keep working hard to make sure the Yankees make the playoffs in 2005.

"When it's all said and done," Alex has said, "I want to go down being remembered as a winner."

Selected Career Highlights

2004 traded to the New York Yankees
selected to his ninth American League All-Star Team

2003 voted the American League's Most Valuable Player (MVP)
became the youngest player ever to reach 300 home runs
(27 years, 8 months)
selected to his eighth American League All-Star Team
led the American League in home runs (47) for the third straight
year

2002 led the major leagues in home runs (57), RBI (142), and total bases
(389)
voted the Texas Rangers MVP
selected to his seventh American League All-Star Team

2001 led the American League in home runs (52), runs scored (133), and
total bases (393)
became the fourth shortstop in MLB history to lead his league in
home runs
broke Ranger records for home runs, runs scored, and total bases
selected to his sixth American League All-Star Team

2000 hit .316 with 41 home runs and 132 RBI
selected to his fifth American League All-Star Team

1999 selected to his fourth American League All-Star Team

1998 became the third "40–40" player in MLB history,
hitting 42 home
runs and stealing 46 bases
selected to his third American League All-Star
Team

1997 selected to his second American League
All-Star Team

1996 won the American League batting title
with a .358 average
selected to his first American League All-Star
Team

Glossary

American League Championship Series (ALCS): a seven-game series played by the winners of the two American League Division Series. The team that wins four games in the series goes on to the World Series.

batting average: a number that describes how often a player makes a base hit. Major League Baseball's best batters usually hit above .300.

division: a group of teams within a league. Major League Baseball's 30 teams are divided into six divisions. In the first round of championship playoffs, teams play a five-game Division Series.

double: a hit that allows the batter to reach second base safely

draft: a yearly event in which professional teams in a sport are given the chance to choose new players from a selected group

extra innings: additional innings played to break a tie score

free agent: a player whose contract with one team has ended, freeing him to join any team that offers to sign him

home runs: hits that allow the batter to circle all the bases to score a run

line drive: a hard-hit ball that flies straight forward, instead of up in the air or down at the ground

Major League Baseball (MLB): the top group of professional baseball teams in North America, divided into the National League and the American League

minor leagues: leagues ranked below the major league

runs batted in (RBI): the number of runners able to score on a batter's hit, including the batter

scouts: people who watch and judge athletes' skills

spring training: a period from February through March when baseball teams train for the upcoming season

stolen base: a play in which a runner on base advances to the next base without waiting for the batter to get a hit

wild pitch: a throw from the pitcher that the catcher cannot catch. Runners can advance one or more bases on wild pitches.

World Series: MLB's championship, played each season between the best American League team and the best National League team

Further Reading & Websites

Donovan, Sandy. *Derek Jeter*. Minneapolis: Lerner Publications Company, 2004.

Rodriguez, Alex. *Hit a Grand Slam*. Dallas: Taylor Publishing Company, 1998.

Stewart, Mark. *Alex Rodriguez: Gunning for Greatness*. Brookfield, CT: The Millbrook Press, 1999.

Stout, Glenn. *On the Field with . . . Alex Rodriguez*. Boston: Little Brown and Company, 2002.

Thornley, Stew. *Alex Rodriguez: Slugging Shortstop*. Minneapolis: Lerner Publications Company, 1998.

Boys & Girls Club of America
http://www.bgca.org
Visit this site to learn more about Alex's favorite organization, the Boys & Girls Club of America.

Espn.com
http://espn.com
Espn.com covers all the major professional sports, including Major League Baseball.

Major League Baseball
http://www.mlb.com
The official site of Major League Baseball provides up-to-date news and statistics of all 30 Major League teams and every major league player.

Sports Illustrated for Kids
http://www.sikids.com
The *Sports Illustrated for Kids* website covers all sports, including baseball.

Index

Photo Acknowledgments

Photographs are used with the permission of: © Rick Friedman/CORBIS, p. 4; © Mike Segar/Reuters/CORBIS, p. 5; © AP | Wide World Photos, p. 6; © Jeff Zelevansky/Icon SMI, pp. 7, 8; © Gail Mooney/CORBIS, p. 9; © Tom Bean/CORBIS, p. 10; © Classmates.com Yearbook Archives, pp. 11, 13; © David Bergman/CORBIS, p. 12; © Rob Tringali/SportsChrome, pp. 15, 21, 24, 28, 29; © Michael Zito/SportsChrome, p. 16; © Jeff Carlick/SportsChrome, pp. 17, 20; © John Klein/SportsChrome, p. 18; © Nancy Kaszerman/ZUMA Press, p. 22; © Reuters/CORBIS, p. 23; © Ray Stubblebine/Icon SMI, p. 25; © Peter Muhly/Reuters/CORBIS, p. 26; © Shannon Stapleton/Reuters/CORBIS, p. 27.

Cover: © Rob Tringali/SportsChrome